Removed from Invent
Guelph Public Libra

J428.2   Gregory, Josh.

GRE   Adverbs   JUL – – 2014

C.2
Guelph Public Library

Adverbs

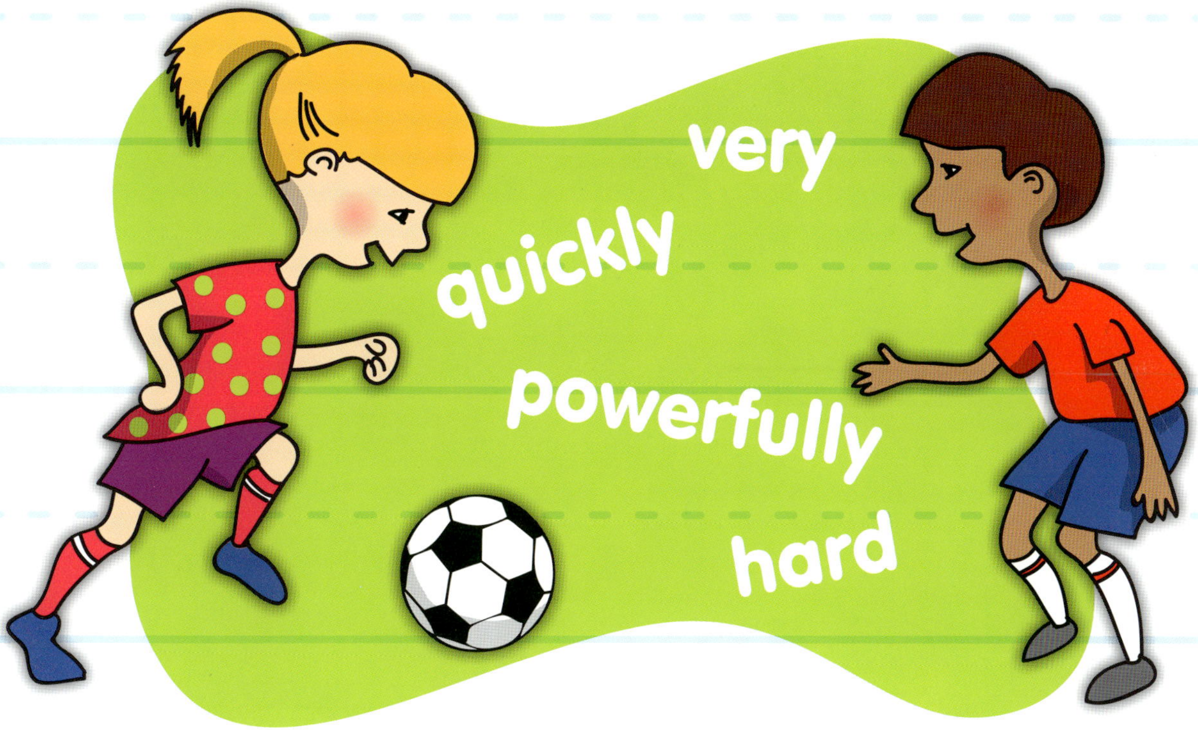

by Josh Gregory

CHERRY LAKE PUBLISHING • ANN ARBOR, MICHIGAN

J428.
2
GRE
C.2

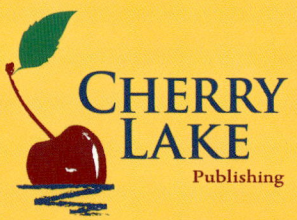

A note on the text: Certain words are highlighted as examples of adverbs.

Bold, colorful words are vocabulary words and can be found in the glossary.

Published in the United States of America by Cherry Lake Publishing
Ann Arbor, Michigan
www.cherrylakepublishing.com

Content Adviser: Lori Helman, PhD, Associate Professor, Department of Curriculum & Instruction, University of Minnesota, Minneapolis, Minnesota

Photo Credits: Page 4, ©Pincasso/Shutterstock, Inc.; page 5, ©MANDY GODBEHEAR/Shutterstock, Inc.; pages 6, 13, 16, and 18, ©Fotokostic/Shutterstock, Inc.; page 15, ©bikeriderlondon/Shutterstock, Inc.; page 20, ©Cultura Creative/Alamy.

Copyright ©2014 by Cherry Lake Publishing
All rights reserved. No part of this book may be reproduced or utilized in any form or by any means without written permission from the publisher.

Library of Congress Cataloging-in-Publication Data
Gregory, Josh.
  Adverbs / By Josh Gregory.
    pages cm. — (Language Arts Explorer Junior)
  Includes bibliographical references and index.
  ISBN 978-1-62431-183-3 (lib. bdg.) —
ISBN 978-1-62431-249-6 (e-book) — ISBN 978-1-62431-315-8 (pbk.)
 1. English language—Adverb—Juvenile literature. 2. English language—Grammar—Juvenile literature. I. Title.
 PE1325.G74 2013
 428.2—dc23   2013007018

Cherry Lake Publishing would like to acknowledge the work of The Partnership for 21st Century Skills. Please visit www.p21.org for more information.

Printed in the United States of America
Corporate Graphics Inc.
July 2013
CLFA13

Table of Contents

CHAPTER ONE
   The Big Game 4

CHAPTER TWO
   The Power of Adverbs 10

CHAPTER THREE
   How to Spot an Adverb 16

Glossary 22
For More Information 23
Index 24
About the Author 24

CHAPTER ONE

The Big Game

A championship match is one of the most exciting parts of a soccer season!

"I just know we're going to win today," Lucy said cheerfully. She watched her teammate Jon lace up his shoes. "Be sure to tie those tightly." Their soccer team, the Blasters, was playing a championship match against their rivals, the Rockets. Lucy and Jon were getting ready to join their team and warm up before the game.

"The Rockets beat us pretty badly last year. This time, I'm going to run so quickly and score so often that they won't know what hit them," Jon said excitedly. "Let's go warm up now. We want to be perfectly ready as soon as the referee blows the whistle."

Lucy kicked a ball over to Jon. Jon stopped the ball and skillfully popped it into the air with his foot.

"Run over there," he said. "I'm going to kick it hard!"

It takes a lot of practice to get good at handling a soccer ball.

Lucy and Jon used many **adverbs** as they discussed the soccer game. Adverbs are words that alter, or change, other words to tell more about them.

"Alright, everybody, gather up," said Coach Burns. Lucy and Jon joined the rest of the team in a circle around the coach. "Are you guys ready to play hard?" he asked. Adverbs can alter **verbs**, such as *play*. "The Rockets are a very good team." Adverbs can also be used with

Good coaches encourage their players to try their hardest.

adjectives, such as *good*. "Their best players can run **incredibly** fast." Adverbs can even make changes to other adverbs, such as *fast*.

ACTIVITY

Locate and List

Locate and list all the adverbs in the following sentences:

"Listen carefully," said Coach Burns. "Our strategy will focus mostly on defense. If we defend properly, we might shut them out completely. We also need to score often, if we can. Yell loudly if you are open so your teammates know exactly where to pass the ball. Finally, let me know if you are too tired and need a break. I will put in a sub immediately. We need to stay well rested in order to win."

Answers: carefully, mostly, properly, completely, often, loudly, exactly, too, immediately, well

To get a copy of this activity, visit www.cherrylakepublishing.com/activities.

Adverbs are a lot like adjectives. Both types of words are used to alter other words and add details. But adjectives are used only with **nouns** and **pronouns**. Even though adverbs and adjectives are different, it is easy to confuse them.

Lucy and Jon watched the Rockets warm up. "Look at number 8 over there," Lucy said. "He sure has a powerful shot."

"He won't be a problem," Jon replied. "I can shoot powerfully, too."

Powerful is an adjective that alters the noun *shot*. *Powerfully* is an adverb that alters the verb *shoot*.

"Do you think we will score first?" asked Lucy.

"I hope so," said Jon. "I want to score the first goal myself!" Sometimes the adjective and adverb form of a word are the same. *First* was an adverb when Lucy used it with the verb *score*. It was an adjective when Jon used it with the noun *goal*.

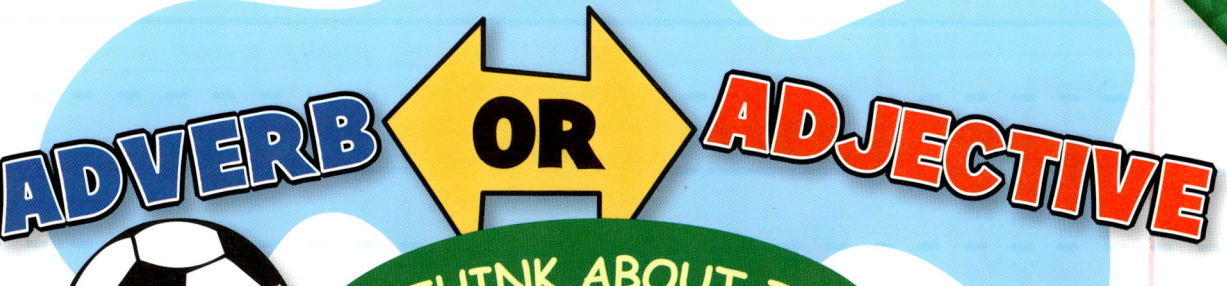

THINK ABOUT IT

Extra Examples

Here are some examples of words in their adverb and adjective forms.

Adverb	Adjective
suddenly It appeared suddenly.	**sudden** It made a sudden appearance.
quickly He ran quickly.	**quick** He is a quick runner.
hard He kicked hard.	**hard** He kicked a hard shot.
recently We recently won a game.	**recent** We won a recent game.
slowly She walked slowly.	**slow** She was a slow walker.
quietly He spoke quietly.	**quiet** He used a quiet voice.
incorrectly They answered incorrectly.	**incorrect** They had the incorrect answer.

CHAPTER TWO

The Power of Adverbs

The referee blew the whistle for halftime. The score was 2 to 1, and the Rockets were winning. The Blasters were down by just one goal. "I feel bad," Lucy said to Jon as they jogged off the field. "The second goal they scored was partially my fault."

"Don't feel too bad," Jon replied. "You weren't the only defender he dribbled past." Adverbs can alter the strength of a verb or adjective. You might say that a soccer team is very good or only somewhat good.

"He went around us so easily, though," Lucy said. "His feet moved so smoothly. I didn't even notice he was faking me out!" Adverbs can also express how something happened. A person might say that a soccer player ran *quickly* or ran *slowly*.

ACTIVITY

Read and Rethink

Read the following sentences. Then rewrite them and fill in the blanks with adverbs you think will work.

"I'm _____ tired," said Lucy.

"Yeah," agreed Jon. "I'm _____ glad it's halftime."

"Be sure not to drink your water too _____, though," Lucy warned. "You will get cramps if you do!"

"Thanks for the tip," Jon answered. "I'll be sure to drink _____."

STOP! DON'T WRITE IN THE BOOK!

To get a copy of this activity, visit www.cherrylakepublishing.com/activities.

11

Lucy and Jon sat down on the bench together. "It was really great when you scored that goal," Lucy said. "I like the way you faked sideways to confuse the goalie."

"Thanks," said Jon. "When Kevin ran ahead with the ball, I stayed behind. Their defenders followed him. That left me wide open for him to pass backward." Adverbs can be used to explain where something happened or in what direction it happened.

"We'll need to score again soon to have a chance at winning today," Lucy replied.

You can use adverbs to explain when different things happened during a soccer game.

"I think we still have a good chance," said Jon. "Our whole team has been playing well recently."

"If we can't pull it off, I'm going to be sad tomorrow," Lucy answered.

"Don't worry," Jon said. "I know we're going to win today!"

Adverbs can also explain when something happened or when it is going to happen.

"Listen up," said Coach Burns. "If we want to get ahead, we need to play more forcefully than we did in the first half. Take your shots less wildly than you were. Aim the ball more carefully." Adverbs can be used to compare differences between two things. The coach used adverbs to compare the way the team played in the first half to the way he hopes it will play in the second half.

"I want the defenders to keep playing as carefully as they have been," the coach continued. Adverbs can also indicate the way two things are similar.

"In the second half, I want you to run the fastest you have ever run. Try the hardest you have ever tried. Now let's go out there and win this game!" In addition, adverbs can be used to compare differences among large groups of things. For example, the coach is comparing this game to every game the team has played before.

Halftime is the perfect time to adjust strategies for the second half of the game.

CHAPTER THREE

How to Spot an Adverb

Soccer teams choose their strongest shooters to compete in shoot-outs.

The game was tied 3 to 3. The referee blew his whistle to end the second half. Coach Burns called the team over to the bench. "What happens now?" Lucy asked him. "We've never ended in a tie before!"

"It's time for a shoot-out," he answered. "We need to choose five players who can shoot calmly under pressure. They need to be players who make their shots dependably. These five players will face off against the Rockets' goalie." There are a few tricks to spotting adverbs. Most words that end in *-ly* are adverbs.

"It's unlikely that all five players will make their shots," the coach added. "But the only thing we need to do is score more goals than the Rockets do." Not all words that end in *-ly* are adverbs. The coach uses *unlikely* and *only* as adjectives.

"Each of the five players will shoot once," the coach said. Not all adverbs end in *-ly*.

Five shooters each from the Rockets and Blasters walked onto the field. They took turns facing off against their opponents' goalie. Jon was the last player to go. The shoot-out was tied at three.

"I'm extremely nervous right now," Lucy said as she watched from the sidelines. An adverb often comes right before the word it alters.

"If he doesn't shoot soon, I'm going to go crazy!" she added. Other times, the adverb comes right after the word it alters.

Shoot-outs are often very suspenseful.

To get a copy of this activity, visit www.cherrylakepublishing.com/activities.

ACTIVITY

Read and Rethink

Read each sentence. Then rewrite it, placing the adverb in parentheses where it makes the most sense in the sentence.

1. Jon touched the ball with the toe of his shoe. (softly)
2. He took a couple of steps back and looked the Rockets' goalie in the eye. (tensely)
3. He burst forward. (suddenly)
4. His kick launched the ball toward a corner of the net. (diagonally)
5. The crowd roared as the ball slid past the goalie's hands. (successfully)

"Don't be nervous," Coach Burns told her. "Jon makes difficult shots often." Sometimes there are several other words in between an adverb and the word it modifies. In the coach's sentence, the adverb *often* alters the verb *makes*.

Winning a soccer championship is a great feeling!

The team chanted Jon's name loudly. They lifted him on their shoulders. Jon held onto the team's trophy tightly and smiled happily.

"Congratulations!" shouted Coach Burns. "You kids played an amazingly good game. I'm extremely proud of you."

"I was insanely worried near the end," said Lucy. "Luckily, Jon is a great shooter!"

Read and Rethink!

Read the following sentences. Then rewrite them and fill in the blanks with adverbs you think will work.

"Phew," Jon said _____. He and Lucy climbed into his mom's car. "I'm _____ tired!"

"I'm _____ proud of you," Jon's mom said _____. "You guys played _____."

"Thanks!" said Lucy as she buckled her seat belt _____. "We _____ play well, but this time we played even _____ than usual!"

Jon _____ looked back at the field through the window. He smiled _____ as his mom drove away. "What a _____ incredible game!" he said. "Next year we'll _____ win the championship again!"

To get a copy of this activity, visit www.cherrylakepublishing.com/activities.

Glossary

adjectives (AJ-ik-tivz) words that describe nouns or pronouns

adverbs (AD-vurbz) words usually used to describe verbs, adjectives, or other adverbs; adverbs indicate how, when, where, how often, or how much something happens

nouns (NOUNZ) words that represent objects, people, places, animals, or ideas

pronouns (PRO-nownz) words that take the place of a noun or a noun phrase

verbs (VURBZ) words that express actions or states of being

For More Information

BOOKS

Dahl, Michael. *If You Were an Adverb*. Minneapolis: Picture Window Books, 2006.

Fisher, Doris, and D. L. Gibbs. *Hole-in-One Adverbs*. Pleasantville, NY: Gareth Stevens, 2008.

Heinrichs, Ann. *Adverbs*. Mankato, MN: Child's World, 2011.

WEB SITE

Walk the Walk Charades
http://printables.scholastic.com/content/collateral_resources/pdf/00/SPB00_015.pdf
Get instructions for a fun game to play that will help you learn more about adverbs.

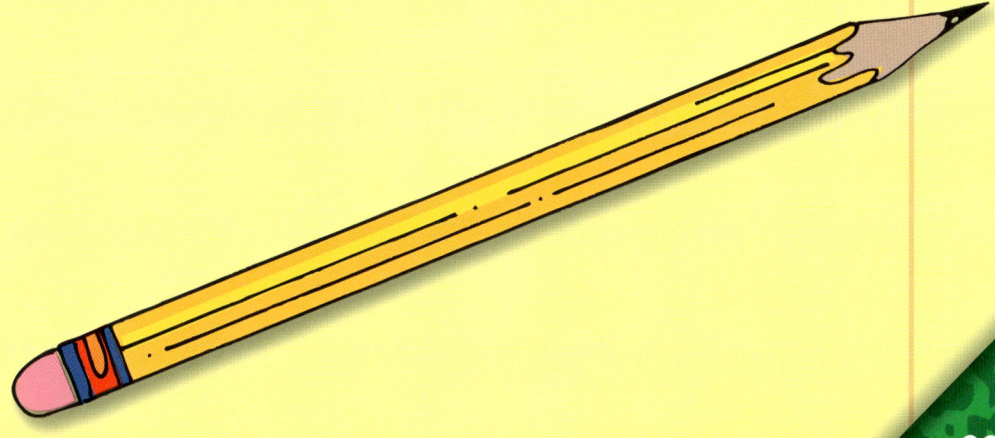

Index

actions, 11, 12, 13
adjectives, 7, 8, 9, 10, 17

comparisons, 14, 15

endings, 17
explanations, 12, 13

differences, 14, 15
direction, 12

how, 11

-ly endings, 17

nouns, 8

placement, 18, 19
pronouns, 8

sentences, 7, 11, 19, 21
similarities, 14
spotting, 17, 18, 19
strength, 10

verbs, 6, 8, 10, 19

when, 13
where, 12

About the Author

Josh Gregory writes and edits books for kids. He lives in Chicago, Illinois.